WHO WOULD WIN?®

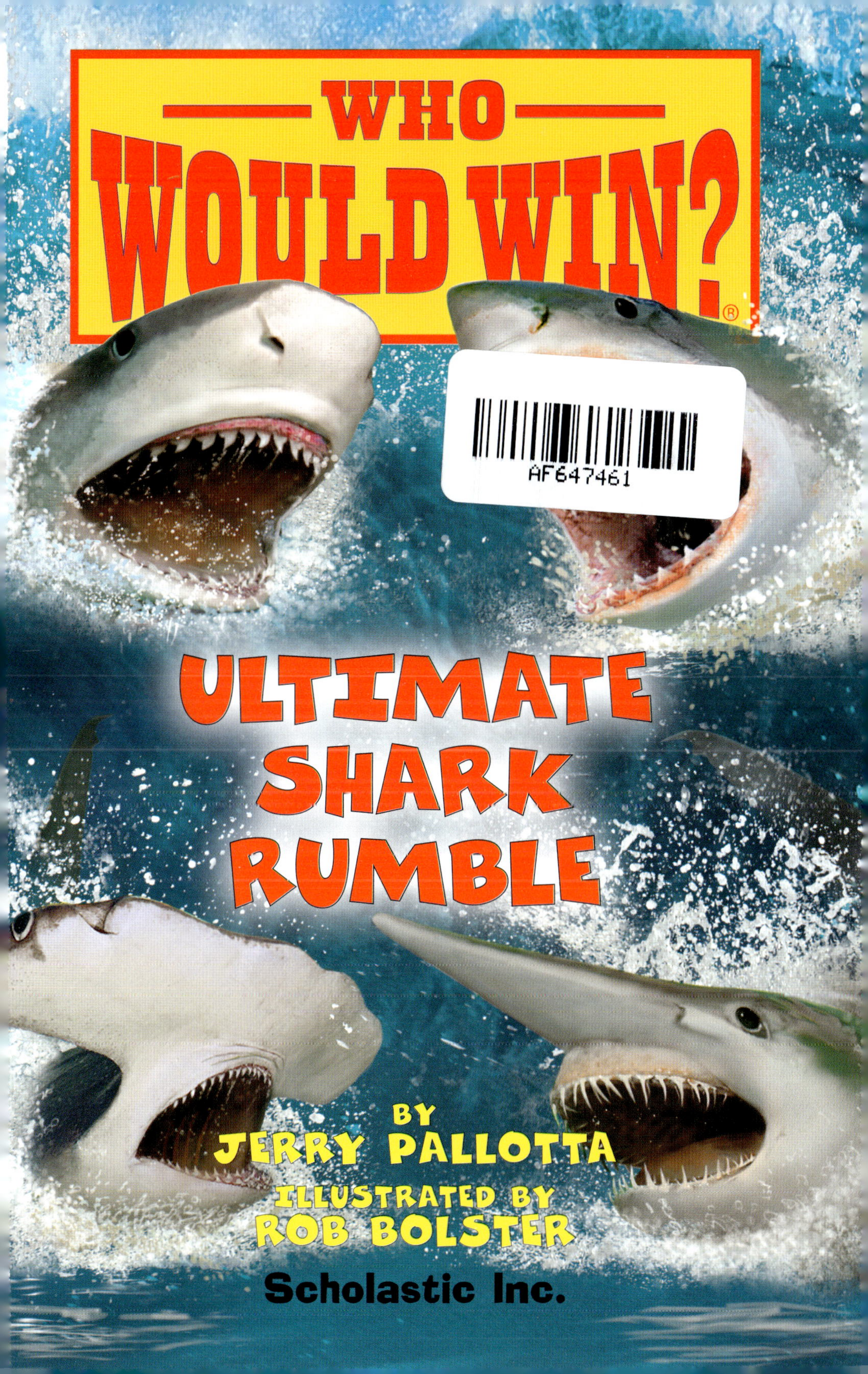

ULTIMATE SHARK RUMBLE

BY
JERRY PALLOTTA
ILLUSTRATED BY
ROB BOLSTER

Scholastic Inc.

16-SHARK BRACKET

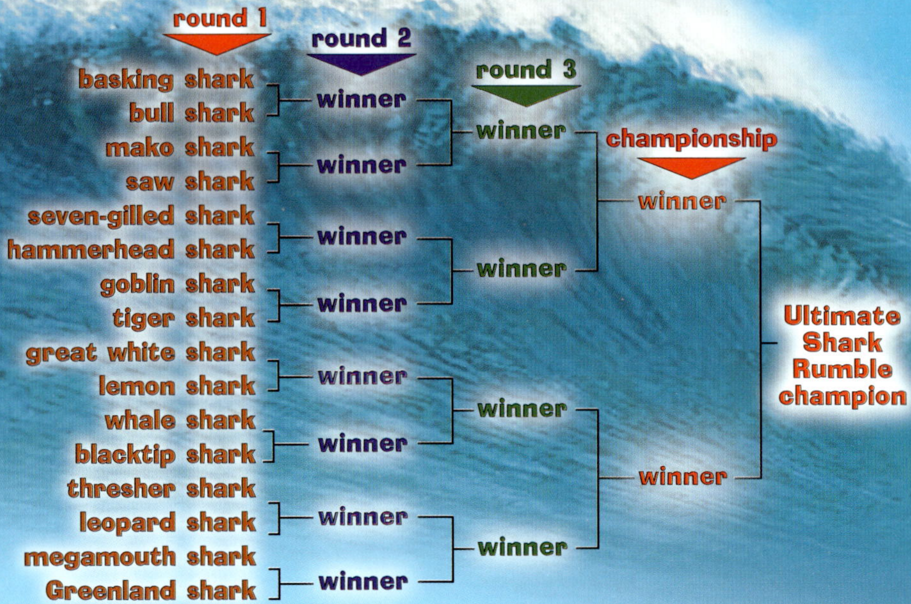

To Andy Pallotta, the great white shark, and Kathy Pallotta, the cookie-cutter shark.
—*J.P.*

To brother Ed Griffin, for his generosity and biting wit.
—*R.B.*

ISBN 978-93-5471-183-1

10 9 8 7 6 5 4 3 2 1 20 21 22 23 24

This reprint edition : September 2024

Printed in India at : VK Global Digital Private Limited

What would happen if 16 sharks were invited to a contest? What if there was a bracketed fight? Who would win? If a shark loses a round, it is out of the competition.

FACT
The basking shark is the second largest fish in the world.

NAME FACT
The basking shark got its name from basking in, or lying in, the sun.

The basking shark is a filter feeder. It swims with its mouth open near the surface of the ocean. Don't be afraid. It has teeny, tiny teeth.

ROUND 1

BASKING SHARK VS. BULL SHARK

MATCH 1

The bull shark is a man-eating shark. It moves in shallow water, where some people swim. It also swims up rivers and sometimes into lakes. The bull shark *does* attack people. Beware!

STRANGE FACT
Bull sharks live well in captivity.

No big teeth? Only a filter-feeder jaw? The basking shark does not stand a chance. The bull shark's strong jaw and sharp teeth bite chunks out of the basking shark. Good-bye, basking shark!

FISHY FACT
All sharks are fish.

TRUE STORY
A bull shark that swam up a river in Africa got eaten by a crocodile.

BULL SHARK WINS!

The shortfin mako shark is the fastest shark in the ocean. It can swim up to 45 miles per hour. Makos are often called the "cheetahs of the sea" or "falcons of the ocean." It is nice to be able to outswim your enemies.

FACT

Sharks do not sleep like we do. They have active and rest periods. For example, reef sharks rest on the bottom of the ocean.

ROUND 1

MAKO SHARK VS. SAW SHARK

MATCH 2

The saw shark has teeth along its nose. It is an easy shark to identify. It uses its nose to slash at a school of fish. How would you like to have teeth on your nose?

LANGUAGE FACT

The word mako *means shark in the Maori language.*

The saw shark is scary looking, but it is no match for a mako. The lightning-fast mako swims right at the saw shark and bites its tail off. The saw shark is wounded and cannot swim.

MAKO SHARK WINS!

Mammals have lungs. Fish have gills. Almost all sharks have five gill slits on each side of their heads. True to its name, the seven-gilled shark has seven gills.

FACT
Sharks do not have bones. Their skeletons are made of cartilage, the same kind of material in your nose.

ROUND 1

SEVEN-GILLED SHARK VS. HAMMERHEAD SHARK

MATCH 3

Its head doesn't look like a hammer to me. It looks more like an airplane wing. When people see that shape, they know exactly what kind of shark it is.

HAMMERHEAD FACT
Its eyes are positioned to have excellent vision.

FACT
One kind of hammerhead shark is known as a bonnethead.

The hammerhead has excellent vision and can see backward. It is watching the seven-gilled shark's every move. When the seven-gilled shark makes a wrong turn, the bigger hammerhead attacks. One bite! Two bites! Good-bye, seven-gilled shark.

FACT
There is also a rare six-gilled shark.

HAMMERHEAD WINS!

The deep-water goblin shark has a scary-looking "double" face. This shark species has been on Earth for more than 100 million years. Its ancestors probably had fights with plesiosaurs and dinosaurs.

RARE FACT
Few goblin sharks have ever been caught.

FOSSIL FACT
A plesiosaur is an extinct ocean reptile.

ROUND 1

GOBLIN SHARK VS. TIGER SHARK

MATCH 4

Meet the tiger shark. It has the perfect name. Surfers and swimmers beware! The tiger shark is known for attacking humans. It has teeth capable of biting tough sea-turtle shells.

SPECIES FACT
A sand tiger shark is a different species than a tiger shark.

This fight is a matchup between an ancient, ugly shark and a sleek, beautifully designed fighting machine. The tiger shark has a larger tail and bigger fins, and it can swim faster and turn better than the goblin shark. The fight does not take long.

SPIRIT FACT
Some Native Hawaiians believe that tiger sharks are the spirits of their ancestors.

TIGER SHARK WINS!

FREE-RIDE FACT
Shark suckers are fish that attach themselves to sharks. They are also called remoras.

The great white shark is one of the most famous sharks in the world. It has a huge, strong jaw with triangle-shaped, serrated teeth. It gets blamed for the most attacks on humans around the world.

FIN FACTS
Sharks have pectoral fins, dorsal fins, pelvic fins, anal fins, and caudal fins.

ROUND 1

GREAT WHITE SHARK VS. LEMON SHARK

MATCH 5

This shark has a light yellow color. Wow—it is different. It has two dorsal fins.

COLOR FACT
Not all sharks are gray.

The lemon shark puts up a good fight, but the great white shark is too big, too strong, and too ferocious for the lemon shark. The great white shark swims right at the lemon shark and uses its powerful jaw to bite the lemon shark. The big bite is fatal.

GREAT WHITE SHARK WINS!

The whale shark is the largest and longest fish in the ocean. It grows up to 40 feet long and weighs up to 20 tons. It has tiny teeth and is a filter feeder. The whale shark swims with its huge mouth open. It strains, or catches, small sea creatures such as krill and copepods. Strange but true: The biggest fish eats the tiniest creatures.

FACT
The whale shark is not a whale. Like all sharks, it is a fish.

MOUTH FACT
A whale shark's mouth is up to five feet wide. It looks like a giant vacuum cleaner.

ROUND 1 WHALE SHARK VS. BLACKTIP SHARK MATCH 6

The blacktip shark got its name from the black tip on its dorsal fin. Blacktip sharks are aggressive. They move toward human swimmers.

It's just not fair—an aggressive shark against a filter feeder. The blacktip shark is not intimidated by the size of the whale shark. It swims and bites at the whale shark. Bites, bites, and more bites. The blacktip shark wounds the bigger whale shark.

The whale shark loses too much blood. It slowly sinks. It will be a giant meal for hundreds of other fish.

FACT

A whale shark is the largest vertebrate animal on Earth that is not a mammal.

DEFINITION

Vertebrate *means an animal with a spine.*

DEFINITION

A whale fall *is when a whale dies and sinks to the deep bottom of the ocean. There, its skeleton becomes a home and dinner for other sea creatures.*

BLACKTIP SHARK WINS!

The thresher shark has a long tail. Its tail is more than half the length of its body. The tail allows it to swim, turn, and stop faster. It hunts using its tail to whip at schools of fish.

FACT
Common thresher sharks are also called fox sharks.

ROUND 1

THRESHER SHARK VS. LEOPARD SHARK

MATCH 7

The leopard shark is a small shark that has leopard-like spots. It grows to only about four feet long.

SMALL FACT
The dwarf lantern shark is the smallest shark in the ocean. It is only about eight inches long.

COOLEST NAME
The tiny cookiecutter shark cuts little cookie-shaped chunks out of other fish, dolphins, and whales.

The thresher shark circles the leopard shark to check it out. There is a huge size difference between this pair. The thresher shark uses its big tail to whip and stun the leopard shark. Its unusual tail is like a secret weapon.

LANGUAGE FACT
In Spanish, a shark is called el tiburón.

THRESHER SHARK WINS!

The megamouth is a big, long shark with a wide mouth. This rare deep-water shark was discovered in 1976. Don't be scared. Big mouth. Big lips. No big deal! This shark is also a filter feeder.

RARE FACT

Few people have ever seen a living megamouth shark.

NO CONFUSION

Don't mix up the megamouth with a megalodon, the largest shark that ever lived. The prehistoric megalodon is extinct.

ROUND 1

MEGAMOUTH VS. GREENLAND SHARK

MATCH 8

Greenland sharks are also called gurry sharks or gray sharks. They live the longest of any shark—between 300 and 500 years. That's a lot of birthday parties. The Greenland shark belongs to a shark species that has been on Earth more than 100 million years.

TRICKY NAME

Gurry are the parts left over after you fillet, or debone, a fish. Gurry is often used for crab and lobster bait.

The megamouth usually eats tiny fish and krill—it wouldn't know how to attack the Greenland shark. The Greenland shark swims toward the megamouth. The hungry Greenland shark attacks the megamouth.

BUMP FACT
Some sharks bump first to try to figure out what a creature or object is made of.

FACT
Greenland sharks have been found swimming one mile below the ocean's surface.

The megamouth has lots of teeth but they are small and useless in a fight like this. The Greenland shark chews up the megamouth.

GREENLAND SHARK WINS!

We're at the end of the first round. Only eight sharks are left in the competition.

The bull shark fought a filter feeder to get into round 2. Now it faces speed and sharp teeth. This is a challenge. Who will win? Who will get into the SHARK FINAL FOUR?

ROUND 2

BULL SHARK VS. MAKO SHARK

MATCH 1

The mako is so fast that the bull shark has trouble finding it. The bull shark has trouble chasing its opponent.

ATTACK FACTS

Some sharks attack from below. Other sharks attack from above.

Speed is a great weapon, but eventually the mako has to confront the bull shark. The bull shark is too strong and too nasty for the mako. The bull shark overpowers the mako. The bull shark has a stronger jaw!

BULL SHARK WINS!

Some people thought the hammerhead might end up in the championship match against the tiger shark, but they must meet in the second round.

ROUND 2

HAMMERHEAD SHARK VS. TIGER SHARK

MATCH 2

TAG-ALONG FACT

Pilot fish get protection and leftover food by following sharks as they swim.

The hammerhead has a smaller mouth than the tiger shark The tiger shark glides to the side and bites off one of the hammerhead's eyes. The hammerhead is in trouble. The tiger shark then bites it in the back.

TIGER SHARK WINS!

Could the great white shark eat every other shark in this book? Too bad the extinct megalodon isn't around to swallow the great white shark with one bite. The great white shark starts swimming toward the blacktip shark.

TAIL FACT
Sea mammals have horizontal tails. Almost all sharks have vertical tails.

ROUND 2 GREAT WHITE SHARK VS. BLACKTIP SHARK MATCH 3

The blacktip shark sees the great white shark and realizes this is a serious contest. There is no place to hide.

PACK FACT
Blacktip sharks are often found in large packs, or groups.

The great white shark attacks. It hides its eyes as it opens its huge jaw and wounds the blacktip shark. The aggressive blacktip shark wants to escape but it's too late. It becomes lunch.

GREAT WHITE SHARK WINS!

The thresher shark, with its fancy tail and tricky turns, tries to intimidate the Greenland shark. Its strategy does not work.

ROUND 2

THRESHER SHARK VS. GREENLAND SHARK

MATCH 4

The Greenland shark is bigger and not scared. It is ready to show off its strong jaw.

DENTAL FACT

A shark loses thousands of teeth during its lifetime. It grows new ones to replace them. Humans only have 32 adult teeth.

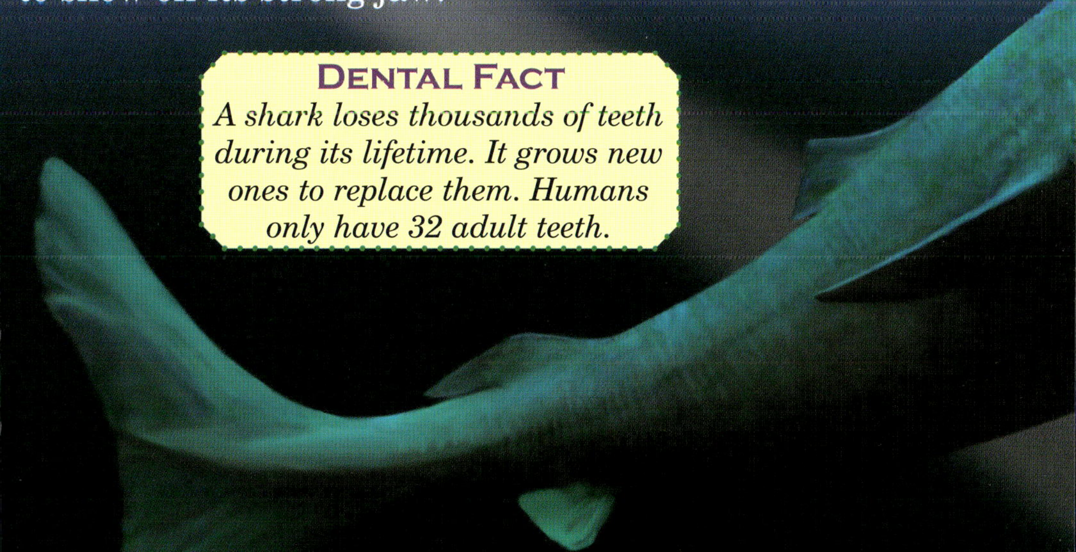

When the thresher shark swims near, the Greenland shark bites a chunk out of the thresher shark.

The thresher shark is overcome by the Greenland shark's strength. Don't mess with an old pro!

GREENLAND SHARK WINS!

That's it! The SHARK FINAL FOUR is set. Bull shark, tiger shark, great white shark, and Greenland shark! All the filter feeders are gone.

There are only four competitors left. Should we call it ROUND 3, FIGHT 1? Or the Semifinals? Oh, right! It's the

SHARK FINAL FOUR

This is a fight of almost equals. Both are ferocious sharks. Each is considered a "man-eater." The bull shark and tiger shark are often in the news.

ROUND 3

BULL SHARK VS. TIGER SHARK

MATCH 1

The bull shark approaches the tiger shark. The tiger shark goes after the bull shark. The tiger shark is longer and heavier. The bull shark is broader.

This is a serious fight. Someone is going to get hurt. The tiger shark overpowers the bull shark. *Crunch!*

The bull shark slowly sinks.

TIGER SHARK WINS!

The great white shark waits for the Greenland shark to swim toward the surface. They are about the same size. The great white shark is a faster swimmer. Its teeth are bigger and sharper.

ROUND 3

GREAT WHITE SHARK VS. GREENLAND SHARK

MATCH 2

The Greenland shark is not as agile, or able to move as quickly, as the great white. The great white shark is more intelligent. What is the great white's strategy?

MOVIE FACT

The great white shark starred in four famous movies: Jaws, Jaws 2, Jaws 3-D, *and* Jaws: The Revenge.

At full speed the great white shark attacks from below. *Crunch!* It rips the soft underbelly of the Greenland shark. The great white shark knew it did not want its first bite to be against the Greenland shark's tougher topside. Good-bye, Greenland shark!

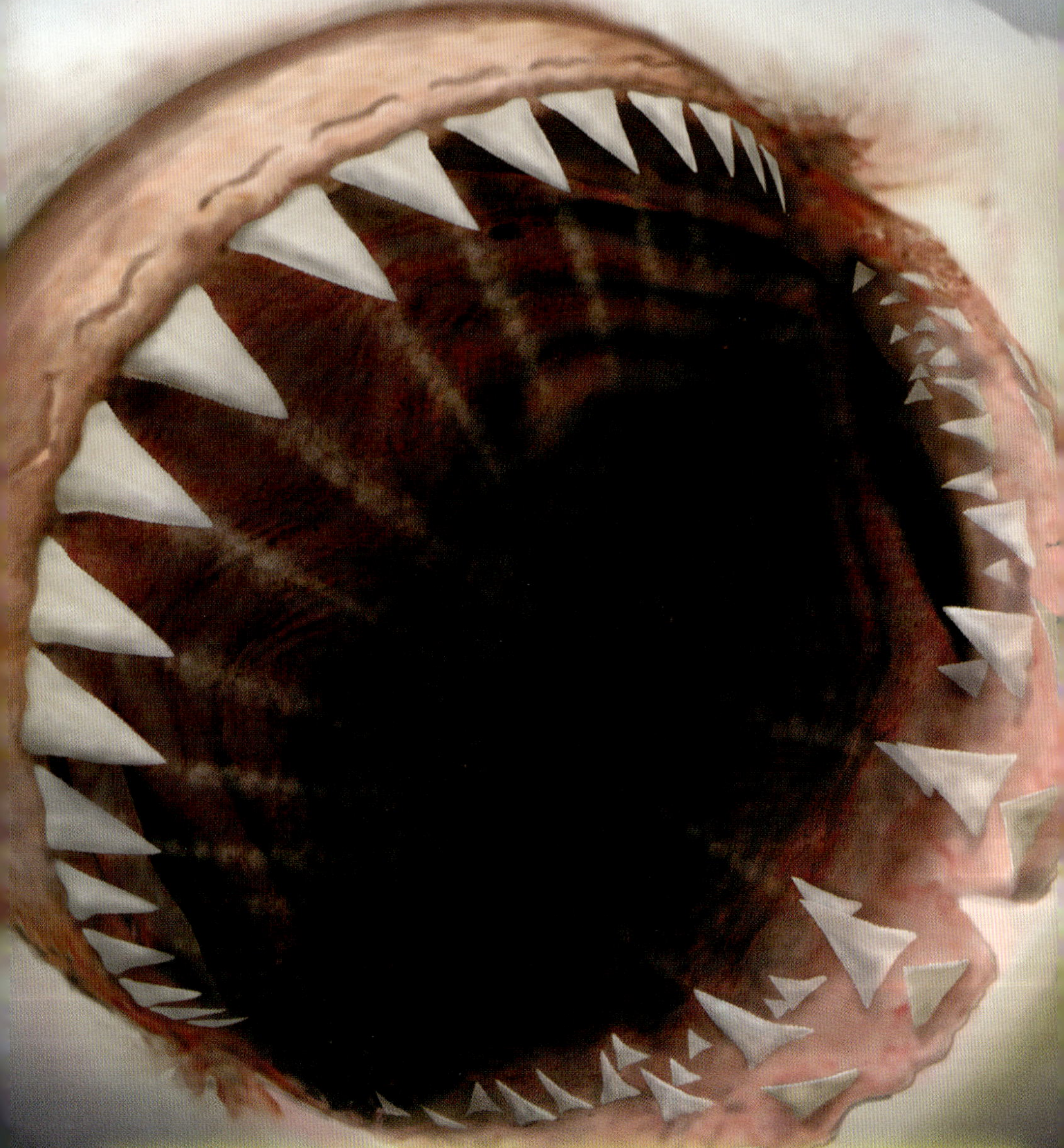

GREAT WHITE SHARK WINS!

We should have known the movie star great white shark would make it to the finals!

CHAMPIONSHIP MATCH!

TIGER SHARK VS. GREAT WHITE SHARK

Two ferocious sharks battle back and forth. Tiger shark versus great white shark! A blunt head against a pointy head. Eyes on the side versus eyes up front. A square jaw confronts an oval jaw.

The great white shark tries to attack from below. The tiger shark stays close to the bottom. As the great white swims by, the tiger shark, with its longer tail, makes a quick turn and bites into the great white. The great white shark is bleeding.

The tiger shark is skinnier than the wide great white. In most fights, a great white shark would win, but today is different. In this battle, the tiger shark is a better warrior.

TIGER SHARK WINS!

This is one way the competition might have ended. Write your own ending or think of a new version of an Ultimate Rumble book.